ONE ATOM TO ANOTHER

One Atom to Another

Brian McCabe

POLYGON
Edinburgh

This edition first published in Great Britain
in 1987 by Polygon, 48 Pleasance, Edinburgh,
EH8 9TJ.

The publisher acknowledges subsidy from the
Scottish Arts Council towards the publication
of this volume.

ISBN 0 948275 22 7

Typeset by EUSPB, 48 Pleasance,
Edinburgh EH8 9TJ.
Printed by Martins of Berwick

Acknowledgements

Some of these poems have appeared in: Chapman; *The Kingfisher Book of Comic Verse*; Lines Review; The Literary Review; *New Writing Scotland*; Phancy; Paper; Quarto; Radical Scotland; New Edinburgh Review; The Scotsman; Green River Review; National Book League 'Writers in Brief' No. 22 and in *Spring's Witch* (Mariscat Press, 1985) and have been broadcast by Scottish Television.

The author would like to thank the Scottish Arts Council and Stirling District Council for a fellowship which gave him time to complete this book.

For Frank

Contents

One Atom To Another

Noah

Don't talk to me of violence corruption
the imagination of man's heart and so forth
does not interest me I am a practical man
My inspirations come in cubits I deal in lists
of livestock fowl every creeping thing
I know of no Grace unless it is this
a talent for obedience for survival
Let me take a look at the blueprints
a window here a door there whatever
the specifications I will carry them out
to the letter Who am I to question
the merits of gopher wood the dimensions
or the destruction of all flesh No
my business is not to scan horizons
for that I use the raven the dove
If sacrifices are required I will make
sacrifices I have worked with animals
All will go in fear of me no matter
in the meantime my instructions are clear
be fruitful multiply I will do my part
replenish the earth leave it in my hands
A deluge so there will be a deluge
I am a family man I know nothing
of deluges I say nothing wish for nothing
but a quiet life perhaps a vineyard
I did not ask to be a prototype
So be it We have made our covenant.

To Make

Something pure but not pure
as the driven snow
which is muddied by usage
the heavy feet of multitudes

Something like water maybe
though water is seldom pure
the idea of water is purer but
what thirst could that quench?

Is there a gift that isn't
wrapped in its definition
and tied in the ribbons
of giving?

A baby's first breath except
it contains the wheeze of experience
a rattle of its history a restless
ghost of its gasping ancestors

Even a man who is said to be pure
evil has a seam of mirth a glint
of irony an inkling of insight
in short is polluted

I make up a starless night
to mean the mood I'm in or
compare a woman's warm body
to a goddess or a loaf of bread

To sift the trash of the word
to use our impure senses
to find the elements
to make

Something pure maybe this time
it will be pure as pure
as chaos was before
we made our order of it

In the Skip

Half a dozen bricks
are clinging to their brickness
and to the idea of being
a wall.

Drawers lean on drawers as if
their crazy staircase could recall
the time it was a kitchen cabinet.

A mattress, doubled up, yearns
to yawn, stretch, turn over and
scratch itself where it's ripped.

Dust, yes there is dust.
And sometimes I think
my history is there in the skip:

a gap that was once for sitting on;
a piece missing its jigsaw;
a smatter of glass, convinced
it was always meant to be a window.

I peer into the rubble to see
what's salvageable.

CANAL IN WINTER

How can water go into *a coma*?
Or exhaust-pipe with raised head be
a snake in a catatonia —
having swallowed a silencer?

Is a stick, stuck to its stickness,
like anything else I've known?
Why must I create a resemblance
of pram-frame to exoskeleton?

All I know is I must: try again,
with a mind that's frozen over,
to thaw each thing from its name
although it's a doomed endeavour:

through a lens of ice I try
to see the world new again,
as a mother and child pass by
and I hear myself named, Man.

The Seventh Sense

All talk of the Sixth
or of the Five
— none speak of the Seventh.

The Seventh sense can please itself
about what it apprehends:

the grey taste of a rainy day;
a premonition of an aroma;
what the caress once whispered
to a threadbare emotion.

The Seventh sense can dress
in whatever it can dream.

But like the moth who dreamt
she was an emperor
the Seventh sense is never very sure
that it exists.

That's why it keeps reminding us
— with the kiss of a snowflake,
with the colour of a shout —
that we do.

Who knows —
even the diligent earth
might forget to go on turning
if not for the Seventh sense.

Making Senses

A cloud has given up trying to be
an early nineteenth-century shipwreck.
Below it, smoke from a bonfire of leaves
is queuing up into a questionmark:

What, no wind? And it seems to question me:
with these pieces of a black, white and pink
jigsaw, what other picture can you see
but cows? Does the evening stoop to drink

its own shadow, or the beauty queen of trees
tremble, get ready to drop the pretence
of that multicoloured hair-do of leaves?
I am a man and I make my man-sense

of a cloud, the smoke, some cows and a tree.
But no landscape can make sense of my me.

Five Murders
(Found in the *Edinburgh Evening News*)

1.
The dead girl is going on holiday
with her family next July.

2.
Following the discovery of the body
police sealed off the quiet street
and bones were placed around
her purple Morris Marina.

3.
The accused was unable to appear personally
having fallen recently from a church steeple.

4.
In his alleged confession
he told of going to Inverkeithing
for a Perry Como style haircut
in an effort to disguise himself.

5.
On the evening of the killing
he had gone into the garden
to look at his Dahlias.

He saw the hammer
and picked it up.

POST FESTIVAL

The Castle has disappeared
— who unplugged the projector? —
leaving no silhouette
on the night's dark screen.
It's time to start saving
electricity and souls:
at the foot of the Mound
the only street-theatre is
a fanatic waving a bible,
crying his wares: guilt, sin
and the end that's been nigh
since the beginning.
In a wind-stirred litter
of tickets, omen of autumn,
a lone newspaper-seller stands
offering the Late Late Final
to the last despondent clowns
on their way to Waverley Station
in the perennial rain.

The Snowmen

Into the silence of that night —
so we went, together and alone:
to be the mute adults we were
and to listen
to all the children hullabalooing
and to watch
as they slid down the thrilling dark
ice of that night — their sledges trays,
tin lids, car mudguards, anything . . .
And seen between tenements, the moon
(our steps had cramped to a stop)
looked distant, fragile, precious . . .
Then rounding a corner, we saw
another moon of snow loom towards us —
behind it, two teenage boys
who stopped, leaned on it, smoked
like men loused from work.
Was it that tamed satellite
there in our street
made us feel the living strangeness
of our own bound planet?
The sky was thick with meteorites
and those trees, unsure of their roots,
had pushed out glinting, winter buds
and had grown a sudden ghost of fruit . . .
Was it that cast the spell?
We stared at the streetlight
where particles whirled
into brief definition then blurred . . .
You teased me to say what they were like.
Fallout, I thought, then said confetti.

No not confetti, molecules. No not . . .
And then we saw them, the snowmen:
assembled, smiling, there

in the shrouded gardens, they were
the presiders over that night then.
Was it our mood made them ominous?
But what could they portend?
As if they waited, watched us . . .
And I remember them:
assembled, smiling, there
they are waiting, watching us go
into the silence of this night —
so we go, together and alone.

Shoes in a Charity Shop

Why don't your cratered faces
ever seem to sing, as the moon's does?
Or laugh, with swelling cheeks, like hers?
Enough of your always yawning mouths.
You are too full of emptiness for me.
Too twisted with human histories
of caved-in cheeks, lolling tongues.
You remind me too much of the men
who have worn themselves out in you
and of those you will choose again:
by whose beds you will wait for morning
like misfortune itself, open mouthed.
I'd forgive you your leathery senilities
and even the disgust you inspire
if you did not so much smell of charity
to the well-heeled volunteers.

It Was Not Just

a denuded tree a ravaged forest
an eye locked in a socket of ice
not just those delicate horrors
skeletons of birds for example
glued to the iron earth no
it was not just our winter
baring its teeth in the usual way
what was it then what was it
that bowed our heads as we waited
clung like a cold sweat to our coins
made us less than naked in our clothes
between our eyelids it slid
veiled our sight with its ignorance
inevitably it leaked into our minds
blotting thought
it seeped at last into our hearts
extinguishing feeling
                                        what was it
it was not just that winter no
that winter did not cause it
call it our poverty our hardship
in any case it was not just that

DESCRIPTION

from the frayed mouth of a coatsleeve
the empty hand held out

with its lifeline like any other
from birth to death

nothing more to be said about it
no poetry for that hand

the best description of poverty
is money

Enemy

I will never forgive you for what
your towerblock has done
to my skyline.

On my summery path, you've thrown
the world's photograph —
torn in half.

Among your chemical jetsam
is a gull with glued-shut wings.
As is the future.

Will you face yourself at last
when I hold your mirror up
with all its cracks?

No, you'll turn from it, hoping
the deformed unborn don't count
your mistakes on their twisted fingers.

The Harbour at Dunbar

I return with my seaweed of ideas —
all those sea-smoothed smithereens
poets search among for meanings
with words honed down to pure sound
by a wind that's keen on 'keening'.
All those images of rusting hulls
holding up their slender crucifixes
and of plump, kazooing gulls
in smooth white polo necks.
Sprawled by the harbour wall,
that spaghetti of ropes and nets.
A boy who'd been dipping his pail
stared at the sea, spoon by spoon —
so I dip into the day's recall
and stare at it, until
my mind is as empty and silent
as an out-of-season hotel.
Then I remember, late into the night,
the swastika that crawled up on a wall
trailing its message:
'KEEP SCOTLAND WHITE'.

Cat

Looking up from what I'm doing
(looking up a word, to find out
if it means what I *want* it to . . .)
I find out it's me who's been
looked up — by the unexpected:
outside my window, looking in,
is a striped Astonishment.
I see myself as I'm seen
by this startled incarnation:
in his eyes' mad, golden moons
there is terror — and recognition.
And I see what I mean to him
whether I want to or not:
Man, in his undergrowth of words
hunting a wild connotation.
As I close the curtains on him,
he turns on his tail's questionmark
and leaps into a starless, dark
night full of desperate definitions.

Grey Squirrel

Accused by my interest, you start —
squirreling to your feet — and let fall
the evidence, in a chestnut shell.
You place both hands upon your heart
as if to say I've got the wrong guy.
Take it easy, I too have survived —
therefore guilty.

And know the Fall, a hasty scarper
among the dying and the discarded
for what's to be hidden and hoarded.
What's to keep the keen teeth of winter
from meeting in my throat? I'm aware
of what conscience is to the survivor —
something to hide.

So I'm studying you, to discover
how to freeze, become an illustration
in a book thought suitable for children
before bewildering my own tall accuser
with the smokescreen of my tail as I flee
— no doubt up one of those open-mouthed trees
with raised eyebrows.

made a north star out of silver
paper glue and glitter and so
when we all come on we'll know
where the stable is because
that's where we've to stand and
Mary says her doll will fit
the cradle it's just a box maybe
we should get some hay maybe
some animals Joe's got a rabbit
but I don't know if they had them
in the bible anyway the other two
are Melchior and Balthazar and
I got chosen I'm one of the three

I'll need a striped dishtowel
some frankincense and a bethlehem

Children's Art Exhibition

'Primary'

We can step back but never into
those depthless gardens
never go down that vertical path
through a land of primal flowers
to the house which is also a ship
leaning over a bit in the wind
a flag in every window
a roof-red sail
step back but never understand
how a tiny chimney can trail
its mammoth smoke over the sky
but the ship which is also a house
won't take us now won't take us
to the shore of that magic realm
where trees are lollipops a dog
is a blob with terrible teeth
where mummy is a smiling blur
with two blue daubs for eyes
daddy isn't in the picture

'Secondary'

the grey god of diagram stretched out
his HB hand to be studied
and to place that palpable apple
glowing in its pubescent bowl
from now on he'll live on detail

the dry repast
of a cross-sectioned cabbage
a few old shoes
whose laces wriggle to live
nothing fancy
a skull or two

'Handicapped'

meanwhile
wearing only a stuck-on suit
of paste and sugar-paper and
posterpaint polka-dots
the clown with the botched grin
the black crosses for eyes
is still being made to hold up
the swaying big top of it all
on the peak of his dunce-cap
a silver tinselled thing
while wobbling around the ring
on his buckled monocycle

The Message

Little brother I got a message for you
not from Santa no
it's from Da.
Listen will you.

See before you got born
see Da still had a job to do.
We got bacon and eggs for breakfast.
Ma used to afford to get a hair-do.

Then she goes and gets pregnant again
and even although it was by accident
Da said we could maybe still afford it.
He meant you.

It turns out we can't.

The other thing is
this room before you came along
only had the one bed in it.
Mine.

See there isn't really room for the two.
So what with one thing and another
and since you were the last to arrive
Da says you've to go little brother.

Here is your bag it's packed ready
with your beanos pyjamas and a few
biscuits for when you get hungry
I'm sure you'll be better off wherever

you end up so good luck and
goodbye.

A Bedtime Story

There was a bottle with a dream in it.
Da drank from it because
this dream made everything seem
a lot better than they was.

A boring word sounded cleverer
and like it might mean more
and even his jokes sounded funnier
than they ever been before.

The dream it made Da swagger
and laugh and drink up more
till swagger turned into stagger
and laugh turned into roar.

Then the dream turned into a bad dream
and it made Da curse and swore.
So when he got back home at last
well he banged the front door.

See Da in this dream is someone
who knows when he's always right
so when Ma went and argued with him
they started to shout and fight.

They fight about Da and his dreaming
see then the nightmare goes on
he's hitting her now she's screaming
then this morning Ma's gone.

And Da says he can't remember
what the dream was all about.
So he goes out to look for her.
Don't ask me how I found this out.

I'm yer big sister amn't I.
I know things you don't that's all.
Like the story of the bottle with a dream in it
a dream called that's right

now get to sleep.

The Lesson

I'll tell you what now little brother
I'm going to teach you something
you'll never ever forget.

You go half way upstairs that's right.
You turn round you shut your eyes.
You keep them shut tight.

Now on the count of five
now I want you to jump.
Now is that clear.

Don't be scared little brother.
I'll be standing at the bottom here
to catch you so be brave.

Five I said I'd teach you something
this is it don't ever trust anybody.
When you're older you'll thank me for it.

Shut up.

The Visitors

Little brother you'll never guess what.
The aliens have just landed.
No they don't have pointed ears
but they are armed and handed.

No they don't have suckers.
No not red blue yellow or green.
But all in black and silver
and one keeps a talking machine

in a special secret pocket.
You can see the blue light out there
well it comes from their rocket.
You can hear their voices downstairs

they're talking to Da that's right.
They want to know where he was
on the planet Earth last night
between seven and ten because

how should I know?
Ma says they'll go away soon
but if you ask me I don't think so.
I think they'll take Da to the moon.

No they are not friendly.
No you can't go downstairs.
I will protect you don't worry.
Move over.

The Warning

Little brother beware the black car
with the strangers' faces in its windows —
the one they call the Getaway Waggon
taking Da to the job he goes.

Little brother beware the black car
with the iron bars in its windows —
the one they call the Black Maria
taking Da to the jail he goes.

Little brother beware the black car
with the dark glass in all its windows —
the one they call the Funeral Hearse
taking Da to the grave he goes.

Little brother beware the black car
no matter what is in its windows
no matter what they call it
taking Da to wherever he goes.

One day it will come for you.

Four Riddles

1.
unlike the mountain
you must climb it
because it isn't there
until the summit

2.
if you in your little boat
were to row across a wide river
wouldn't you let go the oars
to listen to the water ever?

3.
in the desert a man
is dying of thirst
is praying for rain
by cupping his hands

4.
I do not query the fountain
from its gargoyle mouth spills
something to drink after all
to drink and see the light in

Silence, Here and There

No not hear it exactly but
notice it with the ear —
there in the Beethoven somewhere
at the bottomless bottom of it
is a tiny root sprouting crescendos.
It grows in the mind's room also:
behind that remindering clock,
under the uneasy easy chair — the one
that whines every time you think in it —
silence, here and there
among the brain's furniture.
Then it's the eye looks for it
in another room, the one out there —
as if a silence could be seen
as a clock can, or a chair.
Maybe it can be: over there,
that shape with a hole in it.
A polished, discarded guitar
is a silence for the eye, isn't it?
Or a blank page before
some tiny — but not to it — life
crawled over it and stopped.
And then there's the one
unheard unseen but felt for —
a pulse that doesn't come.
The one to listen for is rarer:
the silence that blackbird is dipping
his voice in when he sings,
the silence of a space in thought
a space from which thought springs.

Narcissus

I made a most precious most rare
mask of my vanity:

the peacocks of its ears
spread out such envious feathers,
each with an eye
and in each eye a mirror —

or rather a secluded pool.
And in each pool was reflected
only my image of me,
till into this cool ear drifted

a rumour of someone other
who had wasted and wasted away
who was also it seems my lover
who became at last less than her name.

Behind this mask I found
a man drowning.

Respectable

There was one mask I did not make.
I inherited it:

worn smooth by the dead generations,
cruel weather and a long tradition
of deceit, its lack of expression
has made it its own definition.

It is featureless — perfectly
untroubled by doubt or dramatica —
it knows no extravagance or frenzy.
It endures.

The world through its pinhole eyes
is colourless quite, but reliable.
Those it won't fit envy it
and so it is enviable.

It is visor, shades, windscreen.
Behind it what dark demon screams?

Demon

One mask was cast in my anger:

from its sizzling ears,
from its zigzagging hair,
sprang the mad fire that meant
nothing.

From its black boiling eyes,
from the flames of its face,
blared the dead stare that saw
nothing.

I wore it here and there
and especially everywhere where
its bared teeth passed
for laughter.

This particular mask was so thin
it was almost transparent.
Apparently no one but I knew when
I wore it.

It had two reversible faces
one of which smiled and was meant
to make everyone think I was
impossibly innocent.

I called it sentimentality.
The sneering side was intended
to make everyone take me to be
so very experienced:

I called this side bitterness.
Unfortunately, there was overlap
and something of a twistedness
in its make-up,

so that each of these faces was
fighting the other always
to be the one everyone saw.
I suffered many reversals.

Behind this mask I found
that truth, too, was reversible.

Sincere

The last mask but one was the one
I wore to the door to greet strangers.
It was interested, attentive
and opaque.

Friends and enemies alike
agreed it was a most authentic fake
and fearing what lay behind it
thought I wore it for their sakes.

It tilted a little as it listened
patiently to all their poetry
or to problems of another sort:
at funerals it was compulsory.

I wore it, on and off, in bed.
My lover examined it with tact
for its fissure its imperfection
but found it grotesquely intact.

She attacked it with her anger:
it cracked.
Smacked it with indifference:
it split.

Touched it with her love:
it shattered.

From my mirror the last mask stares.
I can't really say I wear it —
it goes deeper, layer on layer,
skin within skin. I've shed it

over and over. A painful process —
maybe it's the face I deserve.
Still it clings to me — no less
than the god I won't serve.

I did not make it or inherit it.
Its origins I cannot detect.
I'll strip it again and sever it,
though deep down inside I suspect

that behind this mask I'll find
no one there.

Ulterior Man

I am your ulterior man.
At four a.m. I am
combing the city for clues
as to how my night will end
as to how my night began.

I wander, pause, wait.
Pay attention to this or that
doorway, to this or that
window — the drawn blind
on which the light throws
your eligible shadows.

To no purpose I go
now quick as a busy insect
now singularly slow
and being frankly eventual
I go always *incognito*.

I dine out each night.
To be precise: I eat
what I find in the dark.
If it rains I drink rain.
I do not mind. I get wet.

I avoid back alleys —
afraid that, should
the occasion present itself,
I might attack someone.

I have found my calling
in the night, its fullness, its plenty.
I prefer it to day:
to roam the suburban streets;
to track the moon
through the city's routes;
to watch the great buildings be
dark, momentous, empty.

When I spot a lit window
I note it
with no especial intent
unless it be simply to note.

It is good to be my own man
but there are drawbacks:
it is shocking how quickly
a marriage can collapse.

Sometimes I think:
to sleep through the day
to stay awake through the night
it precludes all opportunity to —
but no, it is better so:
to prowl the world undisclosed
conferring with shadows.

46

Friends accustom themselves
and cease to call.
It is well known I am unavailable
being in conference with the stars
discussing with rat, mouse and owl
how best to overthrow day.

You if you are out late
or extraordinarily early
may see me come towards you.
You will avoid my glance
as we pass.

I am your ulterior man.
I am what you will
always suspect
gave life a bad reputation
among those who felt able
to judge it.

Inner Man

I could say he's the pulse of a star
its light an inkling only
now reaching me — but that
would make him poetic, far from me.

I could compare him to the sun,
but then I'd eclipse him.
Or to a dream I'm waking from,
but then I'd forget him.

Or call him a wild smithereen
of God, who cannot believe
in God — but that
would make him sound ridiculous and holy.

Or tell you that while I talk
he listens — less to the words
than to the endless narration
of rain on my roof.

Describe how he watches the rain
hang beads of light on a clothesline
then spends my money on a necklace
to entice my common-law wife.

O I could say I'm his shadow,
say 'double', say *doppelganger*,
recount all the names I've coined
in the hope that he'd answer.

But all this idle metaphor
would never mean what I mean
by my inner man and so —
and so silence.

Actually,

I shouldn't have mentioned him
but a moment ago
I picked up a river-worn stone
I've kept in a drawer for years.

And I did not know what it was.
I recognised him then,
in the moment of that cool weight
in my palm, and in the notion

of a clean contour the water
had smoothed to a conclusion:
a stone like any other and yet —
one. One.

A Survivor

The brains of a living monkey?
Snake's eyes? A bull's testicles?
He'll eat anything: make soup
of snails; he'll pickle and preserve
all things, ostrich and eel —
all will be shredded, dried or jellied.
The belly of the lamb also.
The feet of the duckling also.
If need be he will make lemonade
of termites; spaghetti
from birch-bark. Ant's eggs,
cats' tails, the slugs of the sea —
O nothing will go to waste.

We have among us a survivor.
Don't trust him.

and all he is is a fat
man lying flat on his back
on the grimy grass of Central Park
with this battered black bowler hat
pulled all the way down over his eyes
and with his belly swelling out of that
waistcoat that just can't be buttoned
string-belted pants open flies
no shoes apparently
a bum apparently
and yet

playing on his trumpet so
Triumphantly

You're stuck in your rut old stag.
You've been domineering the season
too long. How haggard you've grown.
I've amused you before old pro
with my amateur antlering antics.
You'll get a charge out of me yet.
To be blunt, I'm hacked off
with the sight of your proud silhouette
on the lids of all the shortbread tins.
All that Monarch o' the Glen bullshit.
I've been tasting the air between us
and I know that your reek is rank.
All year I've stayed in training
for this clash of horns. Listen.
I'm not all stomp and snort.
I'm no phantom of the mountain mist
nor your image come home to haunt you.
I'm not posing for a post-card. This
is death on the dim horizon. This
is my jagged head you can see
on the ragged skyline. So:

square go.

Future Archaeologist

What notion of yourself will you exhume
when you open that door in the stone
and step into our century's room?
Will our solemn, Tuttankhamun telephone
make you hear the echo of an instinct?
What will you do when you hear the tone
of our antiquated answering machine?
I'm out now. Please say who you are
and leave your mesage — I'll
call you back as soon as I can.
Amazed by what you have been,
will you tell us who you think you are?
Or will you say, 'But we've come so far
since then . . .' Or, as our faces
vanish from the snapshot's catacomb,
'It's as if they are watching us . . .'
don't mistake our carpeted rooms
for a shrine, our beds for our graves.
Future archaeologist, make it known
that we tried to love and be loved —
display our dark, embracing bones.

Autumn

I offer her a cracked landscape a dusty ode,
she goes on sobbing out her story.
In her voice there is the rustle
of a blackbird among dead leaves.
I say Don't. I say Come on
tell her winter might never happen.
Anyway I say you're in your prime.
She shakes her head. She makes
her ear-rings' dark berries dance.
Go on I say. I say Shed
that burden of all your beauty then.
Caress her ear: Though you're no
snowdrop of a gusty budding girl
and wouldn't be seen dead in crocuses
at my party of the year you're still
the one I hope will stay to the end.
So pull yourself together —
now it's time to go but we'll
meet again next year I'm sure.
I survey the final moment of her face
run my fingers through her windy hair
take her ripe mouth's trembling kiss
squeeze the damp leaves of her hands —
before I can say I'll miss you
she turns away.

At a Poetry Reading

The blackboard is dusted of its words.
In the ghostly cloud of what's erased
you can make out the long, greyish faces
of the failed and the minor and the dead.

A good-looking girl (what's she doing here?)
looks dead bored at the end of the row.
Between us there's a very long line
of outnumbering chairs. Let us go

then, you and I, let us leave the great
poet to console: 'The real audience
is always one . . .' But we are too late:
silence closes in. And it begins

with an endless introductory apology
for what we're going to hear. What's more,
the wind in the corridor is doing
something onomatopoeic with the door.

The poetry makes just as much sense.
And we do not listen — so much so
that a latecomer interrupts a cadence
and unwittingly steals the show.

Theatre Critic

What's the play, by the way?
Hamlet, is it?
Godawful plot, but still —
to be or not to be, eh?
Still a very pertinent question.
More so than ever in a way:
very worrying this nuclear business.
What I say is:
everyone ought to have a shelter,
not just civil servants and royalty.
To tell you the truth I don't care
for Shakespeare — makes me depressed.
Some good speeches though: whether
'tis nobler in the mind to suffer . . .
I can never remember the rest.
A CND production I see — as if we
didn't have enough on our plate.
These alternative people make we weep.
To tell you the truth, I hate
the theatre — I'd give it up, but
it's the only place I get any sleep.
Too old anyway — I've reached the age
of Claudius, too late to make amends.
In any case, I know how it ends:
bodies all over the stage.

Cheers.

Figure in a Landscape

The painter is long past his heyday
now he follows a wavering line
into a world of grey

No one takes him seriously even he
knows the canvas has defeated him
so be it

The colours were always too bright
brushes too bristling with their own
busy life the world was never so impasto

Still the smell of turpentine hangs about
like the pungent ghost of something
his talent maybe his cowardice

Who knows maybe he'll strike out yet
turn his back on the galleries the gaggle
of sincerely indulgent smiles

He'll disappear into a crowd scene
become a figure in a landscape
sketch for a self-portrait

Till death that ultimate abstract
it's been done before of course
frames him in its empty frame

The Blind

The blind old men who come arm in arm
On good-smelling days to the park,
Grateful to the girl who brings them
Since they seldom have the chance
Of a slow, recollective game of bowls.
The sun that signs their faces
With smudge-like marks where eyes were
Suggests to their memories a notion
Of green, and summer days ago.
Taking pleasure from the silence of grass
And the weight of the wood in the hand,
They engross themselves in the game
They play by sound intuition:
The girl is young, sighted.
She stands at the far end of darkness
And claps her hands — once, twice —
And then the first bowler stoops,
As if about to kneel and be blessed,
Then throws to her clapping hands.
As the dark wood is travelling the green
She waits, motionless, and waits
As if by any slight move she might alter
The swing and slowing of the bowl.
When it halts, she bows, she measures,
Then calls its distance, its 'time':
'Seven feet, at four o'clock.'
Again she claps her hands.
Another player stoops, lets go . . .
This time it comes closer, close enough
To enter the young girl's shadow.
When it kisses the jack, there's a 'cloc'.

The old men smile.

This is Thursday

The key argues with the lock
before the ward door is opened
and a male nurse orders me in.
I note the military manner,
the clipped moustache, explain
I'm an old friend of hers
come to visit on impulse.
He nods, inspects my appearance
and suggests that I wait here.
'Here' is a windowless room
where television tells the news
to a range of empty chairs.
A chalked blackboard declares
that this is Thursday.
I wish it wasn't, aware
of the custard-yellow walls
and someone's hand over there —
waving to me, and to no one.
A pale plant starved of light
wilts in its own dim corner.
I ask myself: How could anyone
leap from a tenement window
and land in this dark asylum?
And I wait. Wait for the present
to step out of the past. Then,
across a wasteland of years,
through a fog of sedation,
my old friend looks at me again
with her violated eyes.

I compare the room to a cell
and claim we've locked the world out.
You point out it's that kind of hotel.
I say the collapsed windowblind
resembles a defunct concertina.
You say that won't help us find
a cover for the naked window.
To me, the coathangers' jangle
(it sets your teeth on edge, I know)
is like a skeleton's laughter
and isn't the sink, with its dangle
of chain, a bit of a godless altar?
You point to the drip, eye the stain
and conclude: it won't hold water.
You tell me I'm full of unfeeling
and unhelpful comparisons.
Very well. The crack in the ceiling
reminds me of no far horizon.
These rips in the sheets are nothing
like old men's toothless grins.
But now I need help with something:
how to look into the literal mirror,
nailed above the shelf-like shelf
and find a way not to compare
that half-smiling human error
to this cracked, but shining self.

Hotel Room, Bangkok

How to make love in a cave of mirrors
on this bare bed under that strip of light
to the sound of heavy breathing all night
from an impotent air conditioner?

Above the bed someone's stuck a picture
of a couple in the naked embrace
of a shameless lens — the garden's the place
to take a soft porn shot back to nature.

At least back to the nature of its myth:
in a city where love's only for sale
we've this Adam and Eve to contend with

as well as our own voyeurs. I mean all
these mirror-twins we're going to bed with:
we watch them pluck their fruit, taste our Fall.

A Thunderstorm in New York

'Smoke. Smoke. Loose joints!
Try before you buy, c'mon now brother!
Get wise, get high and get by!
No arty-fishy-al in-greedy-hints!
Smack acid hash grass coke
and all farmer's cuticles!
Toke before you smoke!
Smoke. Smoke. Loose joints!'

And you beat your burden drum
now, and now, in a makeshift city
where the sky is a skin stretched taut:
between the darkness and the darkness
flash your cymbals.

'I is tired man I is tired
I walks all the way uptown
and all the way back downtown
and listen brother I tell you truly
I didn't see nobody around.
No I didn't see nobody around!'

And how that black man howled
and howled all night, in a doorway
on East Second Street: he,
but it sounded wilder than a man,
freed his anger.

'Esscuse me mister mister hey —
could you please help me please?
Cause ma leg is broke see.

See I gotta get up to thee
hos-pee-tal, get ma leg fix.
Esscuse me mister mister hey —
could you please help me please
to get up?

And we in a room above him
while the t.v. told its murders
made our love just as the city
lit up, lit up, then the rain came.
World in sunder.

'What happened — he okay?
SAY MAN — YOU OKAY?
What happened anyway?
He got hit. Did he get hit?
Think he's gonna be okay?
SAY MAN — GONNA BE OKAY?
But what happened anyway anyway
he's still breathing.'

And you beat your burden drum.
And we move to your beat — as trees
thrash in the wind, we too have roots:
between the silence and the silence
breaks your thunder.

He wants and wants with a tidy hand
to write 'not known' on your letters,
steaming open the one you won't send —
he's been holding it up to the light
in an envelope of your skin,
wants to seal it and forward it
with condolences to next-of-kin.
Can't you feel his courtship begin?
He wants everything in black and white.
He's sending you your favourite flowers
and in his kiss-crossed message
can't you read his minus grin?
He's circled your head with a dark halo
in a picture you don't know you're in
and at last he's got your number:
there's a space for it beside your name.
And while you're playing for time,
his rules don't have a game.
He's the one who keeps calling you up
then hangs up when you say hello,
like some jealous ex who thinks no
means yes, he doesn't want you living,
but wants and wants with a dry caress
to find out your body's misgiving:
he will dress your nakedness as nude,
of course he will ask you to dance.
With defunct tongue he'll speak
the dead metaphors of romance,
whispering 'love' when love isn't —
will you cling to his jilted bones?

And His Model

He must have had urgent business
to leave you so soon this morning
as the early light was forming
your features in tenderness.
Apparently he has just gone:
your eye still lingers on

his absence. A white nightdress
reveals your dreaming breast
to be ignored, and blessed
by the heavy gentleness
of your working woman's hand:
the canopy is lifted and

a moment of your nakedness
is there. Later you will share
your love like bread, unaware
that you will be a mere goddess
one day, and men without desire
will nod, mutter and admire

his *chiaroscuro*.

What do you unravel tonight
as your topless and less and less
is loosening? As the spotlight
carves your waxing moons from darkness,
nudity becomes the disguise:
their constellated eyes

died long ago, and cannot guess
that though your movements excite
and enlarge, your true nakedness
is no more a matter for sight
than the woman your waning eyes
eclipse. And you are wise

to wear the dance-routine so tight
that each gesture of slow undress
covers you, joins you with the night
surrounding your bright sexlessness.
Who sees what the darkness implies
in your orbiting eyes?

WHAT WE ARE

The cat sits upside down on the ceiling,
Miaowing at us madly, licking its itch
And playing with the moonlight that's peeling.
I dive deep into your eyes and I catch

The woman your eyes have been concealing —
Blurring with her, we can't remember which
Is which in this underwater feeling.
In the curtainless room your lips enrich,

You mime what your sea's bed is revealing:
Tentacles tendrils tongues and teeth bewitch
As our touches slur . . . Until we're stealing
The truth from each other at last: too much

Love, and too little, makes us what we are.
(And the cat, distracted, outstares a star.)

Muse

This woman has gone and moved in
to the other room in my brain —
the one with nothing in it
except me.

She's been keeping me awake when she
comes through a door in my dreams
and takes me by the hand
and explains

that a tree leaning over water
is really a net to trap stars in,
that the cat in heat is playing
its one-stringed violin.

From her pocket she takes a summer
with a public park in it,
with a snail of a lawnmower trailing
its greener stripe over the green.

Or unfolds a manuscript of snow —
a cryptic script, in Bird's-feet,
and points to a column of characters
and says to me: translate.

I don't know where she comes from
or what she means to imply
or who she is
or why

this woman has gone and moved in
to the other room in my brain
the one with nothing in it
except her.

EXAMPLE

I draw your attention
to this:

in the gridwired glass
of the skylight

that spiderweb crack
traps the sun.

Another example
of pattern and chance

colluding
to make

that hazardous thing
called beauty.

To the Moon

the dead man said to the moon
look at me
and have pity after all

you rock the cradle of the sea
you are popular with lovers
you inspire a bit of poetry
you hang around with sailors

so why not me?
won't you turn my tide
give me back the lunacy
of my brimming blood?

O moon I'll be your man-in-the
give you my grin don't you know
even dry bones crave to be
embraced by more than wind

a glimmer of your sympathy
is all I require to make a start
on my next life moon don't you see
I beg you my love my sweetheart

who needs you more than I?

(but the moon didn't even blink
when the owl flew into her eye
crying who do you think)

To the Egg

the dead man said to the egg
rest assured egg
you can trust in me

let me help you out of your shell
nest I meant

I promise faithfully not to drop you
O no I won't
I'd cross my heart if I had one
and hope to die if I hadn't

or smash you on my honour or whatever
I keep here behind my grin
I give you my word I'd never
crack you on the hard horizon

egg I'll carry you so carefully
deep in my dark socket
you will be my eye and yes I'll see
that first crack in darkness

the sun's yolk spilling on the sea

(but just then the shell broke
and a small voice spoke its first 'me')

the dead man said to the rose

howzabout you and me
going into partnership together
don't blush no seriously
looks like yours need a manager

you know something rose
you remind me of my heart
but for your opening and closing
you could almost be my brain

with you in my skull's hollow
who knows what might take root then
think what sweet and rosy dreams
we'd be millionaires again

so what do you say beautiful
our backer old man time
will provide us with all our capital
he has shares in Maggot & Slime

don't make me get down on my knees
are we in business are we?

(but the rose shook her head in the breeze
and said nothing not even yes
but what's in it for me?)

the dead man said to the grassblade
my my

so we are green are we
and we can stand to attention
and we are so many so many
we can colour in a mountain

blade listen to me
I too have played the soldier
in another infantry
died for king and country and whatever

I know how it feels to be
one brushstroke in the painting
you won't live to see
blade you could be something

stand out from all the others
if you ring my finger and marry me
to the earth your lovely mother
we're already very close as you see

all we need is a consummation
blade you can stand at ease
to give birth to a fresh sensation
be our go-between blade please

tell her I love her that's all

(but the grassblade saluted the sun
as the evening was invading the trees
and stood up straight and tall)

the dead man said to the woodlouse
ahem

sir excuse me
I see you're househunting again
a scandal if you ask me
that a parasite of your calibre
and refined sensibility
should undergo such degradation

woodlouse look no further than me
I've a number of luxury flatlets
mortgageable permanently
detached and semi-detached
in my empty vertebrae

I'll tell you what I'll do with you sir
since you'll need an immediate entry
and time to save for a surveyor
take my skull meantime rent-free
don't thank me it's what I'm here for

on condition that you tell me
what it is woodlouse
what mysterious ability
makes you when you hear the axe
smell the fire and flee

(but the woodlouse was already making tracks
for the rotting tenement of a tree)

A Plate of Good Soup

I don't mean some allusive consomme
whose stock came out of a mythology.
Nor a fervent confessional broth
with its bitter edge of something
that has stuck to the pot.
I'd eschew a thick language stew
— too many wordy ingredients
fighting to be the flavour.
I mean a soup
drawn from the marrow of living
and stirred by a sure hand
exuding the rich aromas
of nourishment
of love.

Yes we'd give almost anything
for a plate of good soup.

One Atom to Another

I don't believe it.
How many millenia is it?
Don't tell me you don't recognise me?
But we were in the same molecule together
— in the soup.
Atom you don't look a day older.
Remember that time we got drunk together
on amino acids? And then we
formed the first protein — O mother,
in those days we lived dangerously.
O I know we got on each other's particles.
We fell out eventually.
Later I heard you'd moved —
working for some new company
called D.N.A.
Me, I stayed in my element.
Don't get around much, but I'm happy.
Almost got hitched, but it
fell apart — to one of the Carbons.
Remember the Carbons?
I always knew you'd be somebody.
I was right behind you all the way
when you crawled up out of that sea
and evolved into what you are today.
How is it in the life industry?
Heard about your breakdown.
Hiroshima. Nagasaki.
You were put under pressure okay okay
you don't have to explain yourself to me.

I'd love to hear your plans, but then
you've got to shoot off now. So.
Great to bump into you again.
Not often I collide with a celebrity.
We should get together more often.
No seriously.

So long.